She Made an Apple Roll

A beloved family cookbook

Katharine A. Boylan

edited by
Linda L Hoopes

Dara Press
2107 N. Decatur Road, #239
Decatur, GA 30033

ISBN 978-0-9987817-3-0

Mother was the only one we ever knew that made a dessert like her Apple Roll. When Uncle Chris ate it he decided that on her tombstone we should write, "She made an Apple Roll."

So I dedicate this collection of favorites to her,

Emma Troutman Boylan,

for she was an inspired and innovative cook, and to

Tell Emmet Boylan,

who was not only a good provider but a lover of good food. Many a time after eating something he enjoyed, we've heard him say, "Emma, you'd better can fifty quarts."

These recipes have been contributed by my sister, Ruth Grooters; my niece, Bobbie Hoopes; by me; and a few came from the generation before me.

Ruth's two sons, David and John were asked which foods they remembered from their childhood. The grandchildren, Linda, Barbara, Carol, and John Hoopes, Susan and Ben Grooters were given the opportunity to suggest their favorites. Probably no one person has sampled all the foods.

These are not exotic foods. Many are the ones families used again and again. Some may have been connected with a special event. But all have proved to be good eating.

Christmas, 1990

Katherine A. Boylan

Contents

Section I

Meat, Chicken, Seafood

Alpine Steak

Pound steak (1½ lb. – ½ in. thick)
Season on both sides with a mixture of
  ¼ cup flour, 2 tsp. salt, ½ tsp. pepper
Brown steak quickly in beef fat – in large frying pan.
Remove meat and lightly brown
  4 large yellow onions – halved
Return steak to pan – onions around edge.
Pour over
  2 cups V-8 juice
Add 1 tsp. Italian herbs
Simmer at least an hour, until meat is tender.

Beef Burgundy

2 lbs. chuck — cut into cubes
2 dozen little onions — or 2 small cans
¼ cup fat
Brown onions in fat, set aside
Brown meat cubes
Mix

2 T. flour	1 tsp. thyme
1 tsp. salt	1 bay leaf
¼ tsp. pepper	1 cup Burgundy
½ tsp. oregano	dash of nutmeg

Place all ingredients in casserole (except onions)
Bake at 325° — 3 hrs.
During last 20 min. add browned little onions
and ¾ cup of sliced mushrooms

Brisket

Make a paste of
    2 heaping T. of dry mustard
    2 heaping T. of flour
    Vinegar
Spread over brisket
Cover paste with sliced onions.
Add some paprika.
Bake at 325° – at least 4 hours.
This is good hot. When cold—sliced thin—it
   makes good sandwiches.
If not buying a whole brisket, try to buy
   the thicker side.

Creamed Dried Beef

Tear 2 to 4 oz. of dried beef into small pieces.
Stir in pan with 3 T. butter.
Add ¼ cup flour, stir until beef is well-coated.
Add milk — about 2 cups.
Stir until it reaches a boil and is thickened.
Always needs more flour than one thinks.
Serve over toast, waffles, or baked potato.
Microwave hint—Heat milk before stirring in.

The above is the Hoopes version. The Boylans would brown the flour.

Japanese Steak and Vegetables

Slice – against grain, ¼" slices 1 lb. beef (flank or round)
Slice 1 large Bermuda onion, paper thin – separate rings
Slice ½ lb. fresh mushrooms
   1 small zucchini into slender 3-inch spears
   1 cup bean sprouts rinsed and drained, fresh or canned
Have all this ready.
Heat 1 T. oil in non-stick skillet
Add the beef and stir-fry 2 min.
Add all remaining ingredients
         and
   3 T. sherry wine
   1 T. sesame seeds
Cook and stir until vegetables are heated through,
but still crunchy.
Serve immediately.   Serves 4.

Lasagna

Sauce
    Frizzle 1½ lbs ground beef with onions
    Add 12 oz. can tomato paste
          2 cups water
          1 small can tomato sauce
          Salt, pepper, garlic, oregano to taste
Cook 1 lb. lasagna noodles
Have ready   16 oz. ricotta cheese
               sauce
               8 oz. mozzarella cheese
Layer noodles, ricotta cheese, sauce, mozzarella
   cheese in lasagna pan
Use sauce sparingly
Pour excess over top
Bake at 375° – 20-25 min.

Macaroni-Beef Puff

Have ready   1 pkg. (7 oz.) elbow macaroni — cooked and drained.
1 pkg. (3 oz.) smoked, sliced beef
½ cup chopped green pepper
2 T. chopped pimento

In 2 quart saucepan
Melt 1/3 cup butter
Saute ½ cup chopped onion until tender
Blend in ¼ cup flour, ½ t. dry mustard, salt, and pepper
Remove from heat, stir in 2 cups milk.
Heat to boiling, stirring constantly.
Stir in 2 cups shredded cheddar until melted. Do not boil.

In large bowl, slightly beat 3 egg yolks;
 stir in sauce, a small amount at a time.
Fold in macaroni mixture.

Beat 3 egg whites until stiff—but not dry; add ¼ tsp. cream tartar
Fold egg whites into macaroni mixture
Pour into 2 quart casserole or souffle dish.
Bake in preheated oven 325°, 50-60 min. or until set.
Serve at once.   6-8 servings.

Meat Loaf

Mother's meat loaf was never as dry as some
Her recipe was always this proportion—
to every pound of meat
add
1 egg
1 cup of bread crumbs
1 cup of liquid

I have found this works well with one exception. When I use ground turkey I don't use as much liquid. Mother used a mixture of beef, pork, and veal. I usually use all beef, but I do like more liquid than most recipes call for.

"Mustards"

Toast bread on one side only.
Spread untoasted side with mustard—be sure to
　　cover all the edges well—to prevent burning
　　when the meat shrinks.
Season the hamburger as you choose—
　　onion flakes perhaps. If low fat meat is
　　used a little water added may make the
　　meat spread more easily. The meat should
　　be about ½ inch thick.
Broil.

　　　　　　I believe David remembered
　　　　　　these.

Philadelphia Hoagies

1 long Italian roll—cut horizontally—opened up—olive oil

Original Meats	Bobbie substitutes
4 slices Italian capicola	boiled ham
4 slices provolone cheese	cooked salami
6 Genoa-styled salami	old-fashioned loaf
4 slices cotechino	Swiss cheese

Layer of finely chopped lettuce
Layer of tomatoes
Splash of olive oil
Salt—pepper—oregano

The olive oil is a must.

Ruth cut the recipe out of the newspaper and sent it to Bobbie. These have been favorites to take on picnics and road trips.

Porcupines

Mix, form into balls, place in casserole.

1½ lb. ground beef	1 cup raw rice
½ tsp. garlic salt	1 T. chopped parsley
1/8 tsp. pepper	½ c. cold water
1 T. grated onion	Dash—ginger

Pour over the meatballs
　　2 cans condensed tomato soup
　　　thinned with
　　1 can milk or water

Bake in moderate oven 30 min. or until
　rice is tender.

Sandwich Supreme

This may be prepared the night before.
Grease large pan, place 6 slices of bread in pan, cut off crusts.
Cover bread with slice of American cheese.
Spread mustard over cheese. Cover cheese with slice of ham.
Cover with 6 buttered bread slices—butter side up.
Mix 4 beaten eggs with 3 cups milk, ½ tsp. salt.
Pour over all—let stand overnight in refrigerator.
Bake at 300° for 1 hour. Serves 6.

—from 2nd Baptist

This was my "company dinner" when I was in Iran.
I don't remove the crusts, and I usually tear the bread into
chunks and put the mustard into the milk. I like chunks of
ham rather than slices. Day-old French bread is especially good.
It can be made and baked as soon as the bread is wet.

Sauerbraten with Left-over Beef

Cut left-over beef roast in cubes
Brown in 1 T. of fat—Remove from skillet
Add   1 envelope brown gravy mix
        2 cups water
Bring to a boil and add
    1 T. instant minced onion
    2 T. white wine vinegar   Mushrooms and
    2 T. brown sugar   peppers may be
    ½ tsp. ginger   added for
    1 tsp. Worcestershire sauce   variation.
    1 bay leaf
    salt and pepper to taste
Stir occasionally. Remove bay leaf.
Serve over hot noodles.

Stroganoff

This is a way to use left-over roast beef.
Cook

     1 T. chopped onion in

     2 T. butter until yellow

Add

     ½ lb. mushrooms (or canned ones)

     beef—sliced thin

     salt

     nutmeg

     1 cup sour cream

Heat—but do not boil.

Chicken Breasts in Sour Cream

    4 chicken breasts

    1 can (3 oz.) sliced, drained mushrooms

    1 can (10½ oz.) cream of mushroom soup

    ½ cup sherry wine

    1 cup dairy sour cream

    Paprika

Arrange chicken pieces in shallow dish so they do not overlap.

Cover with mushrooms

Combine soup, sherry, and sour cream.   Stir.

Pour over chicken, completely covering.

Dust with paprika.

Bake at 350° – 1½ hours.

Chicken (or Tuna) Casserole

1 cup coarsely cut onion
1 cup coarsely cut celery
½ cup coarsely cut cashews
1 can Chinese noodles
1 can mushroom soup
1 can milk
2 cups chicken
3 T. soy sauce
Mix – Cover with crushed potato chips
Bake about an hour at 350°   or
1½ hours at 325°

This recipe was requested
by Ben.

16

Chicken Divan

Bring broccoli to boil—let stand until ready to combine
In baking dish
     Place broccoli
     Cooked chicken
Cover with sauce—
     1 can cream of chicken soup
     1 cup mayonnaise
     ½ lemon – juiced
     A bit of sherry
Sprinkle with shredded cheese
Bake 30 min. at 350°

    If frozen broccoli cuts or bits are used, they
do not need to be cooked.

Hot Chicken (or Turkey) Salad

Make night before.

Saute   ½ cup celery   ½ cup onion
             ½ cup green pepper   ½ cup pimento (optional)

Mix with   2-3 cups diced chicken or turkey
              1 cup sliced mushrooms
              ½ cup mayonnaise

Line greased baking dish with buttered bread squares.
   (Thin-sliced bread cut in quarters.)

Beat   2 eggs
         ½ cup milk

Add 1 can undiluted cream of chicken soup

Layer chicken mixture over bread

Second layer of bread

The rest of the chicken

Sprinkle with grated cheese.

Bake 1 hour at 325°

18

Roasting Turkey

From Mother Hoopes—Very moist—Perfectly browned.
Wash turkey—inside and out.
Salt inside cavities. Put in stuffing.
Put in roasting pan.
Grease top of turkey, and grease inside brown grocery
    bag on one side.
Insert pan with turkey into bag. Greased bag should
    be next to greased top of turkey. If necessary
    slit bag.
Put in cold oven at 375°. Most turkeys regardless of
    size take 4½ hours.

Aunt Mildred's variation—Place turkey in greased bag,
    bag on rack in roasting pan. Bobbie has never
    tried this but Aunt Mildred swore by it.

Sesame-Pineapple Chicken

In baking dish
  1 can of pineapple – chunks or crushed
  Pieces of chicken
  6 oz. can water chestnuts – sliced
  2 T. soy sauce
  Sesame seed sprinkled over – perhaps 2 tsp.
Bake at 400° until tender.
  I usually cook at a lower heat.

This was a Weight Watcher's recipe we
  really like.

Shrimp Creole

Cook
   ½ cup chopped onions
   1/3 cup cut-up green pepper
   in 3 T. oil about 10 minutes
Add
   1 minced garlic clove
   1 tsp. salt
   1/8 tsp. pepper
   2 cups canned tomatoes
Simmer 30 minutes
Add   1½ lbs. cooked, cleaned shrimp
Heat.
Serve with steamed rice.
Serves 4.

Pearl Hoopes liked
   this very much.

Crabmeat Open Sandwiches

6 Holland Rusks
2 small packages of cream cheese—softened
1 can crabmeat (Lately I've used imitation crab)
6 slices peeled tomato
2 T. mayonnaise
1 tsp. Worcestershire Sauce
6 slices Cheddar cheese
Place slice of tomato on each Holland Rusk.
Mix other ingredients except Cheddar.
Pile mixture on tomato slice.
Bake ½ hour at 325°
Top with cheese slice a few minutes before
removing from oven.

When I taught in Shaker I was often invited to a student's home for
luncheon. This was served once and has become a favorite.

Shrimp Newburg

Cook
    1 pint cooked or canned shrimp in
    2 T. butter for 3 minutes
Add
    1 tsp. lemon juice—cook 1 minute
Melt
    1 T. butter
Add
    1 tsp. flour
    1 can evaporated milk—when thickened add
    2 egg yolks slightly beaten
    2 T. sherry
    Salt and pepper to taste

Add the shrimp. Serve at once.

Tuna Fish Casserole

Drain oil from 2 cans of tuna and add to 1 cup bread crumbs.
Add 2 T. lemon juice to flaked tuna.
Arrange in alternate layers in greased casserole:

    the tuna

    6 hard-boiled eggs – sliced

    1 cup or more frozen or canned peas

Melt in top of double boiler –

    4 T. margarine

Add and blend –

    4 T. flour   2 cups milk

    1 cup grated American cheese   1/8 tsp. pepper

    1 tsp. Worcestershire sauce   ½ tsp. salt

Cook over boiling water until hot
Pour over tuna, eggs, and peas
Top with buttered crumbs
Bake at 375° –30 min or until crumbs are brown.

A lady at a potluck supper in Walpole, N.H. sent this to Bob because he so enjoyed it— many years ago.

24

Section II

Vegetables, Salads

Grapefruit Aspic

Soak   1½ T. gelatin in
       1 cup cold water
Dissolve in 1 cup boiling water
Add
       3 T. lemon juice
       ¾ cup sugar
Chill until about to set
Peel 3 large grapefruit—separate into sections.
Add juice and fruit to gelatin mixture.
Chop and add
    ¾ cup chopped celery
    ½ cup shredded almonds
Place in a wet ring mold.

Green Bean Casserole

2 cans green beans – drained
1 can tomato soup
Shredded Cheddar cheese
Mix all together
Bake – medium oven until
      hot and bubbly.

This was a favorite of
John Grooters.

Lasagna Roll-ups

Cook 1 lb. rippled edge lasagna ~ cool
Combine
    4 cups Ricotta (2 lb. container) or creamed cottage cheese
    2 cups (8 oz.) shredded Cheddar cheese
    2 10 oz. packages frozen spinach—cooked—drained
    1 egg
    ½ tsp. salt
    ¼ tsp. pepper
    4 cups spaghetti sauce
Pour 1 cup sauce on bottom of baking pan—13 x 9 x 2"
Spread ½ cup on each lasagna strip to one inch from end.
Roll up jelly-roll fashion.
Place seam-side down in prepared pan.
Pour remaining sauce over roll-ups.
Bake at 350° – 30-35 min.   10 servings.

Layered Salad

Put in layers in large bowl
    1 head lettuce – torn into bite-sized pieces
    2 cups diced celery
    1 Bermuda onion – thinly sliced – separated into rings.
    ½ cup chopped green pepper
    8 slices bacon – crisp, crumbled (optional)
    1 pkg. frozen peas – raw.
    4 hard-boiled eggs – sliced
    1 T. sugar
Spread 2 cups mayonnaise over top – clear to edges
On top – 4 oz. cubed sharp cheese
Refrigerate 24 hours.
At serving time – mix thoroughly, but do not crush.
If bacon is omitted, add salt.
Serves 12-15

Rice Delight

Melt 1 stick margarine
Add 1¼ cups raw rice — stir and
Put in 2 quart casserole
Add   1 can undiluted onion soup — clear kind
        1 can (3 oz.) mushrooms with liquid
        1 can (5 oz.) water chestnuts, also with liquid.
Stir.
Bake — covered — 375° — 45 min. to an hour.
Add water if needed.

This came from our good friend, Janet Tyson.

Squash Casserole

Cook in boiling, salted water about 5 min. – Drain.
    2 lbs. yellow squash, sliced (6 cup)
    ¼ cup chopped onion
Combine
    1 can cream of chicken soup
    1 cup sour cream
    1 cup shredded carrots
Fold in
    Cooked squash and onions.
Combine
    1 pkg. (8 oz.) herb-seasoned stuffing mix
    ½ cup melted butter or margarine
Spread ½ stuffing mix in 12 x 7½ x 2" baking dish
Spread vegetables over stuffing mix
Sprinkle other half of stuffing mix on top
Bake at 350° – 25-30 min.   Serves 6.

Three Bean Salad

1 cup sugar
1 scant cup vinegar
½ cup oil
Mix the above ~ then add
1 can green beans
1 can yellow wax beans
1 can kidney beans
1 small onion ~ red is best
½ cup chopped celery
Let stand 12 to 24 hours
Other beans may be added   or
mushrooms.
Serves 10.   Keeps well.

To Freeze Corn

After shucking and silking, (with brush or coarse
    cloth), drop ears in boiling water.
After water returns to boil, cook 3 to 5 minutes, until milk is set.
Remove from boiling water and plunge at once into ice water.
    (We do this at the cottage because of the very cold tap water.)
When the corn feels cool to the touch remove and <u>drain.</u>
Cut off the kernels and scrape the cobs.
Freeze in small packages as soon as possible, spreading
    out the packages in the freezer.

To serve—thaw, add salt and butter to taste.
Cook in double boiler or microwave so it will not
    scorch. On direct heat it must be watched carefully.
This has been an annual activity at the cottage ~
    often on Labor Day weekend.   Work but Fun!

Section III

Breads, Cookies, Desserts

Apricot Bread

½ cup dried apricots cut in small pieces.
Cook in enough water to cover
until they are soft, not mushy.
Cool, drain, save liquid.

Batter
1 beaten egg
1 cup sugar
2 T. melted fat
2 cups flour
3 tsp. b.p.
¼ tsp. soda
¾ cup fruit juice
(orange juice may be
added to make enough)

Add
   Apricots
   ½ cup chopped nuts

Bake at 350° – 1 hour
         or
   at 325° – 1¼ hours

   This recipe came from
Dr. Zirbes ~ my sponsor
for my Master's degree.

Cranberry Bread

2 cups flour
1 cup sugar
1½ tsp. baking powder
½ tsp. soda
1 tsp. salt
Juice and rind of 1 orange

2 T. melted shortening
2 T. boiling water ?
1 egg – beaten
½ cup nuts
1½ cups chopped cranberries

Mix dry ingredients
Pour juice of orange in measuring cup
Add grated orange rind, and enough boiling water
    to make ¾ cup.
Add egg to o.j. mixture
Combine all ingredients.
Let stand 20 min. before baking.
Bake at 350° – 50-60 min.

Date Bread

Combine:
  1 cup dates, cut up
  1 cup boiling water
  1 cup sugar
  1 tsp. soda

Then add:
  2 eggs
  2 T. melted shortening
  1 tsp. vanilla
  1½ cups flour
  ½ cup nuts
Bake in loaf pan at 325° – about an hour.

The dates need to be soft and mushy. If they are hard bring to a boil. Usually I use a pot large enough to hold the rest of the ingredients. Be certain the date mixture is at room temperature before adding other ingredients.

  This recipe came from Aunt Linnie, mother's sister. She obtained it from her husband's Dutch relatives. I can almost hear her say, "and could those Dutch women cut it thin."
  This is almost a staple with our family. It may be doubled ~ and freezes well. Cream cheese is especially good on it.

Honey Wheat Bread

Mix

    6 cups whole wheat flour

    6 cups white flour

    Dry milk – ½ cup?

    Salt – 2 T. or less

    3 T. yeast

Make a hole in the dry mix and add:

    1 cup oil (corn, sunflower, canola)

    1 cup honey

    4 cups warm water

Mix – then put on board and knead.

Put in greased bowl, cover.

Let rise until double in size.

Punch down – let rise again.

Shape into 4 loaves, let rise.

When Ruth bakes another kind of bread, one of the men is sure to remark, "This is good, but your regular kind I like better."

Put in cold oven.

Bake 1 hour at 300°.

Brush tops with margarine.

36

Aunt Alice's Little Date Cakes

1 cup dates covered with
½ cup boiling water. Let stand.

1½ cups brown sugar
1 cup shortening. (The
   original called for lard.)
3 cups flour
3 eggs beaten one at a time
   into the shortening and sugar
1 tsp. soda
1 tsp. b.p.
1 tsp. mapleine
1 tsp. vanilla
A <u>few</u> nuts

Drop from a
spoon.
Bake at 375°.

(My brother Jerry was around one time—his
comment, "Aunt Alice <u>would</u> say 'a few.'")

Blond Brownies

Mix
    2 cups flour   ¼ tsp. baking soda
    1 tsp. baking powder   1 tsp. salt
Melt
    2/3 cup butter in saucepan
Add
    2 cups firmly packed brown sugar   *Carol asked especially for this.*
    2 tsp. vanilla
    2 eggs, lightly beaten
Add flour mixture gradually ~ mixing well
Spread in 13 x 9" pan
Sprinkle with
    1 cup chocolate chips
    1/3 cup chopped nuts
Bake at 350° – 30 min. Cool in pan. Cut in 48 bars.

Date Pin Wheels

Combine 1 pound dates – pitted, chopped
        ½ c. water
        ½ c. sugar
Cook until thick – stir constantly – 2-3 min. Cool.
Add 1 c. chopped nuts to dates

Cream
        ½ c. margarine or butter
        ½ c. sugar
        ½ c. brown sugar
        Add egg – beat well
        ½ tsp. vanilla
Add
        1¾ c. flour
        ½ tsp. soda
        ½ tsp. salt

Divide dough in half.
Roll till ¼ inch thick.
Spread half of date mix.
Roll like jelly roll.
Wrap – Chill until firm.
Cut in ¼ in. slices.
Lightly grease sheet.
Bake 400° – 8-10 min.

When Dave was in Fla before he went to
Japan he took pockets full of these on his
way to the garage to play ping pong.

39

Frosted Creams

½ cup shortening
½ cup sugar
1 well-beaten egg
½ cup sorghum
½ cup coffee (not hot)
1 ½ cup flour
½ tsp. salt
1 ½ tsp. baking powder
¼ tsp. soda
1 tsp. cinnamon
½ tsp. cloves

Bake in large flat pan

Dad had a pan made for
   mother that was as
   large as the oven.

Frosting
   1½ cups sugar
   ½ cup milk
   1 tsp. butter
   ½ tsp. vanilla
Boil without stirring
until it forms a soft
ball (234° F.)
Cool and beat until of
a consistency to spread
over cake.

Mother's Scalloped Cookies

2 cups sugar
1 cup butter (or lard and salt)
1 cup sour cream
1 tsp. soda
3 tsp. baking powder
2 eggs
1 tsp. vanilla
½ tsp. nutmeg
6 cups flour   (Use as little as possible to roll them.)
Roll out rather thin.
Cut with scalloped cutter.
Sprinkle sugar on top.

Oatmeal Cookies

Combine
  1 cup shortening
  1 cup white sugar
  1 cup brown sugar
  2 eggs
  1 tsp. vanilla

  1 tsp. cinnamon
  1½ cups flour
  1 tsp. salt
  1 tsp. soda

Mix well – then add
  3 cups rolled oats
  ½ cup nuts
  ½ cup – or more – raisins

These keep well—before they are baked. I keep them in the refrigerator and usually bake but one tray at a time so that I always serve fresh cookies.

Chocolate or butterscotch chips may be added.
Drop on cookie sheet. Bake at 375° – 10-12 min.
Makes a large batch.

This recipe came from a neighbor of Ruth. It has become a favorite—especially of Bob.

Seven-Layer Cookies

Place in large, ungreased, flat pan:
    1 cup graham cracker crumbs
    1 package chocolate bits
    1 package butterscotch bits
    1 cup coconut

Pour over
    ¼ lb. melted margarine

Sprinkle on
    1 cup nuts (optional)

Pour over
    1 can Eagle brand milk

Prick with fork to allow to settle.

Bake 35 min. in 350° oven.

This was a favorite of Barbara's as well as of Carol's who asked for it.

World's Best Cookies

Cream –
    1 cup margarine
    1 cup white sugar
    1 cup brown sugar
Add –
    1 egg
    1 cup oil
Beat – then add–
    1 cup crushed cornflakes
    1 cup rolled oats
    ½ cup chopped nuts
Stir and add –
    3½ cups flour
    1 tsp. baking soda
    1 tsp. salt
    1 tsp. vanilla

Form into balls
Flatten with fork
    dipped in water
Bake at 325° – 10-12"
Leave in pan a few
    minutes before
    removing.

These freeze well
    after they are
    baked.

44

Apple Dessert

3 eggs—beaten
2 c. sugar
1 T. vanilla
1½ c. nut meats—chopped
Add
1¼ c. flour
3/8 tsp. salt
1½ T. baking powder
3 c. chopped apples – peeled

Bake in large flat pan in moderate oven – 30 min.
Serve hot or cold.

The original recipe called for whipped cream, but
with all the attention on low fat, La Creme does well.

This recipe came from my friend, Marian Kirsh.
It is good to take to a pot luck.

Apple Roll

In large, flat, <u>round</u> baking dish, cook
      2 cups sugar
      1 cup water
Biscuit dough
      2 cups flour   1 tsp. salt
      2 tsp. baking powder   ¾ cup milk
      ½ cup shortening
Roll out dough (1/2 inch thick). Peel and chop 4 apples.
Cover dough with chopped apples. Sprinkle with cinnamon.
Roll up (as a jelly roll), cut as cinnamon rolls, 1¼ in.
Place in the hot syrup. Put a dab of butter on each roll.
Bake at 375° – until nicely browned, probably 45 min.
Good hot or cold. Best hot.

    Mother served heavy cream—and it was good!
We splurge on calories and weaken half and half a bit.

46

Applesauce Cake

Cream   ½ cup shortening
                1½ cups sugar

Add   2 beaten eggs
                1 cup unsweetened applesauce (thick)
                2 cups flour
                ¼ tsp salt
                1 tsp. baking powder
                ½ tsp. soda
                1 tsp. cinnamon
                ½ tsp. ground cloves

Fold in 1 cup raisins

Bake in 8 in. square pan

350° – 45 to 60 min.

Baked Topping for Fruit

Place fresh or cooked fruit in greased pie plate.

If fresh fruit is used, add ½ cup sugar.

Cream   2 T. butter
½ cup sugar

Add   1 egg, beaten until light, then
½ cup flour

This makes a fairly stiff batter.

Spread over fruit. Bake 30 min. at 375°.

Serve warm or cold. Good with ice cream.

If you're caught and need a dessert this will cook while eating dinner.

From 2nd Baptist

48

Forgotten Dessert

Beat 5 egg whites

Add gradually – then beat until very stiff and glossy,

1½ cup sugar	½ tsp. cream of tartar
¼ tsp. salt	½ tsp. vanilla

Heat oven to 450°

Put mixture in flat greased pan.

When in oven, turn off heat – do not open door until next morning – or at least 5 hours.

Refrigerate after covering with foil.

This may be cut in squares and served with strawberries or ice cream.

May be kept for several days.

Ruth collected this from a high school friend when she went back to Iowa some years ago.

Frozen Torte

1 Sara Lee Frozen Pound Cake
   Slice lengthwise into thin layers. I try for 10.

¼ cup brewed coffee or 1 tsp. instant coffee in
   ¼ cup boiling water.
2 4 oz. pkgs. Baker's German Sweet Chocolate.
   Melt chocolate in coffee over low heat. Cool.
1 cup heavy cream – whipped – added to chocolate.

Assemble the cake with cream between each layer
   and on the outside.
   This is frozen – then wrapped.
   It keeps well and is good to have on hand.

        Need I say in these days of calorie counting
La Creme or Dream Whip is substituted for the heavy cream?

50

Lemon Dessert

Grease 9" spring-form pan.
Line with 2 pkgs. split Lady Fingers.
Beat 8 egg yolks
Add   ½ cup sugar
                Juice of 3 lemons (about ½ cup)
Cook in double boiler until thick.
Add 1 envelope Knox gelatine dissolved in ¼ cup water.
Cool mixture.

Beat 8 egg whites.   Add ½ cup sugar.
Fold into first mixture. Put in mold. Refrigerate.

At serving time, (spring off), top with whipped cream or
        La Creme.

    Some members of the family have requested this
instead of a birthday cake. Me included!

Plum Pudding Sauce

Mix
    ½ cup sugar
    1 T. cornstarch
    1/8 tsp. salt
    1/8 tsp. nutmeg

Gradually add
    1 cup boiling water
Cook slowly until thick
    and clear.
Add
    2 T. butter
    1½ T. lemon juice or
    brandy

Pour hot sauce over pudding and serve.

Mother used to put this over cake that had become a bit dry.

Strawberry Ice Cream Pie

Dissolve
    1 package strawberry gelatine in
    1 cup hot water
Add ½ cup cold water ~ Stir.
Add 1 pint vanilla ice cream cut in 6 chunks.
Stir until melted.
Chill until it begins to thicken and mound when
    spooned (20-30 minutes).
Fold in 1 cup sliced .or frozen strawberries.
Pour into cooled, baked 9-inch pie shell
    or graham cracker crust.
Chill until firm (20-25 minutes).
Trim with whipped cream and strawberries.

Fruit Jello

Red Jello — (Cherry)
Drain 1 can fruit cocktail—
Add enough water to make the required 2 cups liquid
After Jello is dissolved
Add
     fruit from can
     cut up bananas
     and any other fruit—fresh or canned
        (chunk pineapple, mandarin oranges,
          peaches, pears, etc.)
Serve with yogurt sweetened with sugar or
     artificial sweetener, and vanilla.

                         Ben asked for this.

Lazy Daisy Oatmeal Cake

Pour 1½ c. boiling water
  over 1 c. uncooked oats
Cover ~ let stand 20 min.
Beat ½ c. softened butter
or margarine until creamy
Gradually add

| 1 c. white sugar | 1 tsp. vanilla |
| 1 c. brown sugar | 2 eggs |

Stir in oat mixture.
Mix – then add
  1½ c. flour
  1 tsp. soda
  ½ tsp. salt
  ¾ tsp. cinnamon
  ¼ tsp. nutmeg

Bobbie multiplies this
recipe by 1.5 and
uses a 9 x 13 in. pan.

Bake
  9 in. greased-
    well-floured
    square pan
  350°–50-55 min.
  Do not remove
  from pan.

Frosting
  Combine
    ¼ c. melted butter
    ½ c. brown sugar
    3 T. light cream
    ½ c. chopped nuts
    ¾ c. coconut
Spread over cake.
Broil until bubbly.

55

Orange Date Cake

Mix and bake in well-greased tube pan – 1 hour – 350°

1 cup sugar
1 cup butter
2 eggs
1 package dates–chopped
1 cup nuts–chopped

2½ cups flour
1 tsp. baking powder
1 tsp. soda
½ tsp. salt
1 cup sour milk
Grated rind of 2 oranges

When the cake goes into the oven squeeze the juice
from the 2 oranges and add 1 cup of sugar.
Stir often to dissolve the sugar.

About 10 min. after cake is removed from oven
pour the orange juice with the sugar dissolved in it
over the cake. Let it cool in the pan.
Keep refrigerated.

This came from Minna–my one-time teacher,
co-teacher, and long-time friend.

Sour Cream Coffee Cake

Cream
    1 stick butter or margarine
    1½ cups sugar

Add
    2 beaten eggs
    1 cup sour cream
    ½ tsp. vanilla

This is particularly nice when baked in a tube or bundt pan.

    ¼ tsp. salt
    2 cups flour
    1 tsp. baking powder

Beat until smooth
Pour ½ batter into greased and floured pan.

Combine and sprinkle half over batter in pan –
    ½ to 1 cup chopped pecans
    4 T. brown sugar
    2 tsp. cinnamon
Pour in the rest of the batter – then top with the nut mix.

Bake 45 min. at 350°.

French Pecan Pie

3 egg whites—beaten until stiff
Gradually add
    ¾ cup sugar
    ¼ tsp. cream tartar
    22 Ritz crackers—crushed by hand—not too fine
    1 cup chopped pecans

Place in buttered tin. Bake 30 min. – 300°

Top with La Creme or whipped cream.
Shave chocolate on top.

The meringue may be made the day before.
This is an easily made but very pretty dessert
    to bring to the table.

Pumpkin Pie

For one pie — mix:

    2 eggs — slightly beaten
    1 ½ cups pumpkin
    ¾ cup brown sugar
    ½ tsp. salt
    1 tsp. cinnamon
    ½ tsp. ground ginger
    ¼ tsp. ground cloves
    1 can undiluted skimmed milk

When given the choice of a pie or a Jack-O-Lantern, David, as a young boy, chose pie!

Pour into a nine-inch unbaked pie crust.
Bake 15 min. at 425°. Reduce heat to 350°
— and bake until toothpick comes out clean
when inserted near the center.

When cool top with whipped cream or La Creme.

Section IV

Miscellaneous

Baked Pineapple

2 cups chunk pineapple in juice. (20 oz. can)
1 cup grated cheddar
2 T. honey
½ tsp. vanilla
1 T. whole wheat flour
1 cup whole wheat bread crumbs
1½ T. margarine

Mix pineapple and cheese in 2 quart baking dish.
Mix juice, honey, vanilla, flour, and cook until thickened.
Pour over pineapple and cheese.
Top with crumbs. Dot with margarine.
Bake 30-40 min. at 350°

This is good to serve with ham.

Candied Grapefruit Peel

Cut peel in narrow strips.
Cover with cold water. Boil 20 min. Drain.
Do this 3 times.

Boil for a bit
1 cup sugar
½ cup water

Mix
1 cup cooked peel
1 cup syrup

Boil very slowly. All the syrup will be absorbed.

Roll in granulated sugar.

Cleland's Cranberry Juice Cocktail

½ gallon cranberry juice
1 cup orange juice
¼ cup lemon juice

For syrup cook together
½ cup sugar
½ cup water
2 or 3 whole cloves

Cool and combine with juice.
Add ginger ale and ice.

Each year the Clelands had a Christmas Sing. Bob led the singing and Ruth played. One year they rather insisted Bobbie attend and Ray was persuaded by his mother. That is where they met. Within about six months they were married. And we are glad.

Cranberry Sauce

Grind cranberries — and measure.
Grind an equal amount of apple.
Mix and add sugar — cup for cup.
Let stand a few hours before serving.
Keeps well in refrigerator.
Mother specified Jonathan apples but
   other kinds are fine. They do not
   need to be peeled.

Linda's note: this is a regular part of our
Thanksgiving menu. We call it "family cranberry"
and many family members still use old-fashioned
metal grinders to make it.

Fondant

Mix
  3 cups sugar
  1 tsp. cream tartar
  1½ cups water

Stir well before putting on to boil, but <u>not</u> while cooking.
Wipe sides of pan often with damp cloth.
Cook until soft ball is formed in end of spoon when
  dipped in cool water.
Pour into platter.
Let cool until candy wrinkles when platter is tilted.
Beat with pancake turner until it sugars.
Knead and form into balls after adding color and flavoring.
Top each ball with a half nut meat.

Mother put peppermint in the white, wintergreen~pink.

About Thanksgiving time mother started candy-making. It was put in
the unheated spare bedroom to ripen. She made such smooth fondant. How
much easier it would have been had she had a thermometer.

Pickled Cherries

Fresh sour cherries (pie cherries)
Cider vinegar
Sugar

Wash and pit cherries. (A hairpin works well.)
Cover with vinegar in a large crock. Soak at least 24 hours.
Pour off vinegar. (Will be red but can be used.)
Measure cherries.
Alternate layers, cup for cup, of cherries and sugar in crock.
Cover lightly. Stir gently once a day until all sugar
is liquefied.
When no more sugar crystals remain, place in jars, cap.
Delicious with lamb, beef, etc. After the cherries are
gone, the remaining syrup is good for basting ham.

This recipe comes from Ray's mother, Pearl Hoopes.
We've all enjoyed it.

R & K Cereal

In large bowl mix
5 to 10 cups of rolled oats
1 cup each of
   sesame seed
   sunflower seed
   wheat germ
   soy flour
   dry milk
   almonds – cut up
Add
   1 cup oil
   1 cup honey
Let stand a few minutes
until it is all coated.

Bake in roasting pan at 275°–never more than 300°. Stir periodically until a golden brown.

As soon as it comes from the oven stir in a cup of raisins.

This is an adaptation of a recipe Ruth and I (R&K) found in the fall of 1971. It has been used almost constantly since then.

Toasted Cheese Roll-ups

1 loaf Very Thin-sliced Bread
Cut off crusts — use rolling pin to flatten slices.

Fill with following mixture —
   8 oz. grated, extra sharp cheese
   Grated onion to taste
   Enough mayonnaise to moisten — not runny
   Hot sauce to taste.
   ½ stick margarine — melted

Freeze. When ready to serve cut each roll into 4 pieces.
Sprinkle with paprika — salt if desired before baking.
Bake at 375° until toasted.

Thin-sliced loaf — 30 slices.
8 oz. cheese for one loaf.

These are good to have in the freezer for unexpected
   guests.

Recipes

Section I: Meat, Chicken, Seafood

Recipes

Recipes

Notes

Made in the USA
Columbia, SC
17 February 2024

31673346R00055